MW00655198

CHOOSE YOUR OWN BEGINNING

by Amy Saul-Zerby

Be About It Press

Be About It Press

@baipress

November 2022

ISBN: 978-0-9986012-8-1

cover design by Larissa Erin Greer

edited by Alexandra Naughton

CONTENTS

TRUST THE PROCESS

are you sleeping
enough

are you eating

maybe we should
look into
a SAD lamp

maybe we should
consider

fish oil

maybe we should
think about

adding an anti-
depressant

maybe we should
cut back on

the anti-depressant

how long have you
been feeling like this

how long have you
been feeling

how long have you
been   like this

how long have you
been   this

I CAN LET ANYONE INSIDE ME IF I WANT TO

can fuck you without
either of us taking off
our shoes & pretend like
it didn't happen.

i could never do what you do
says a stranger after
the reading. says
you're very brave

i don't bother telling her
that i'm not really, i've just
been thru so much worse
than stage fright

HOT GIRL SUMMER

i can't tell you
what to do but
i won't let
that stop me

don't start
with me if
you don't plan
on finishing
with me

for god's sake

shy dreams about
a fernet cocktail

i dream of ice cream
wake up hungry,
indulge

life is short
eat dessert first
et cetera

INFINITE COLLAPSE

the kindest person
i ever dated

in reference to
my illness

said 'i love you
anyway'

nothing is
collapsing

that hasn't
collapsed

a thousand
times before

EVERY DAY IS A FUCKING SNOW DAY

love is not writers block
which bends w the remover
to remove

no, poems are an ever
fixed mark that looks
at me like it wants
to fuck me against a wall

calm down, this is
not shakespeare

calm down, we are not
making art here

it's snowing so hard
that i feel less bad about
not leaving the house

snowing so hard that
today i'm like everyone else

NOT TO SPEAK OF HOW THE BODY

becomes a home becomes
a prison. not to linger in the

doorway *(on which side)*
of one's own trauma. i am trying to

tell you it's ok without lying.
trying to cut through the same noise

but differently and yes, it is
impossible thank you for asking

TEXT ME MEMES EXCLUSIVELY

text me twitter
screenshots

text me you
got home safe

text me you
are still there

i just want
to know

you're still
there

FREE DRINKS & BAD ADVICE

joke about how you never should've
been born: hold for applause

try to dictate how people touch you
& act surprised when it backfires

teach yourself to like avocado
so everyone thinks you're normal

don't count your lovers
for fear of diminishing them

don't kill any birds with any
amount of stones

people who live in glass houses
carry no moss. if you try

sometimes you might find
you get what you need

I AM TRYING TO SOLVE
THIS I PROMISE

desire is a
thing w which
i cannot
be trusted

the nearly
impossible
is the most

important if i
believe
it to be

god, i am so pure
in my endless
fascination w ghosts
& the act
of believing
i'm a person

can't see
thru this
but why not
keep trying
forever

no such
thing
as fragility
anyway

i can't
believe
i'm not
better

yes i can
yes i can
yes i can

THE TRUTH LIES

the truth rewrites itself like
everything is magic
except for me, you think

it is going to be okay but it
already is. i am unmade so i
unmake myself over +

over. a building is torn down
to make room
for another building. the strongest

selves are built on memories
of pain. patron saint
of silver linings, bless me:

i think i forgot who i am
on purpose. i think i might
not want to wake up.

OKAY, FINE

draw a line in the sand
& i'm still the same

there is something
to be said, but i'm not
the one to say it

the fabric tears because
it was made to

teach me to breathe
from my diaphragm
if you want

i will turn this poem right
around, let you out on
the side of the road

inside my head there are not
voices but there could be

as the old adage says, don't
count yr blessings before
they hatch

IN WHICH JENNIE'S CAT TRIES TO CLIMB ONTO THE FRIDGE

leaps onto
the counter, singes
her paws on
the stove & retreats
under the couch
to nurse
her wounds

we google what to do
to prevent a cat
from doing this.
there must be plenty
of cat owners with
electric stoves, i say.

she asks her roommate
if she wouldn't mind
placing a pan filled with
water on the stove
after using it

a trick among
cat-parents
to keep their children's paws
unscathed, a type
of baby proofing

there isn't really much else
you can do

the cat wants
to get up there
it does not know whether
the stove is hot

i text a man i loved
an erotic poem, wish him
a happy belated
national orgasm day

ain't a good poem until
someone dies,
says the man

in the poem, the couple
die connected

this is my only model
for love:

when my grandmother died
my grandfather said
he didn't want to be here
without her

a month later, he was gone

so when you ask if i am tired
of nursing
my own wounds:

of course i am.

don't i, too, want someone
to connect myself to before
i die?

it isn't that i don't

i just don't think
it will make me any less
afraid
of dying.

JFC

this is brutal
trying to fly but
idk today

o, my lost suitcase!

quiet love of
my fucked up life

i'm in it until i'm not
in love w

the idea of myself
but also not at all

god forgive me for ever
haven't wanted

to swallow you
don't want to be scared

anymore but the world is
still here, you know?

SHOW ME THE WAY TO GO HOME

for louise

on a day when i can barely leave
my bed let alone my house

i think of how you found joy
in almost everything

re-read your letter, written at 3am
because you could barely contain

your eagerness to be awake,
in which you write that you cannot

believe how much you like pulling
weeds from your garden, the sense

of power it gives you to pull one
almost your size from the earth

i think of watching as these simple
joys were stripped away by age,

one by one. dig up a letter in which
you talk about how much you like

to watch the snow settle on the birch
trees outside your window. search out

a column you addressed to me on
the occasion of my birth, welcoming

me to the world and all the wonder
it would offer me. i know you would

not blame me for not being able
to feel it sometimes. but you are

not here to tell me so, and i miss
you immeasurably, and i think

i need very badly to hear you say
that this is all right, that it isn't

my fault, that you are still proud.
when we lost you, for the first

few years after, i would wake in
the night and swear i could see

you, and was not afraid. louise,
i don't believe in ghosts and i was

taking my medication and this is maybe
the only way i can think to explain it

to love someone so deeply, and be
loved in return is a kind of magic

i forget i ever believed in. that kind of love,
it does things to the brain, even to my

half-broke one. is it any wonder i fixate
on the idea of finding it again. louise,

i know i will never find it again. i don't
need you to tell me this is all right.

it isn't, and it is. you're here and
you're not. if i can ever forgive

myself for not seeing the wonder
you hoped i would, it will be because

i know you would want me to. to look
at snow on trees and find joy, for me

may be too much of a stretch, but
to look at them and think of you

& find joy in the thought? louise,
i don't believe in a god but your love,

it did things to my brain, and this—
i can't think of any other way

to explain it—is a kind of magic
even i might still believe in.

AFTER THE AFFAIR, or THE LITTLE MERMAID POEM

listen: i want to know
how to change
the story, i think

i can figure it out
someone writes
that anxiety is just

a conspiracy theory
against yourself
& they're not wrong

i conspire against
myself daily
i mean, my brain

conspires, i mean
i conspire against
my happiness like

i am more comfortable
on the ground
safer at rock

bottom other shoe
can't drop if you never
take a step kind

of thing but it's getting
colder i mean i'm
getting colder i mean

it's getting to take
a toll on me. when i was
younger i had an

illustrated copy of The
Little Mermaid in
its original form

pre-disnification, where
she is not only mute
but each step she takes

on her new legs, she feels
as if she is walking
on knives, and i am so

much quieter than i
want to be & when i saw
the Disney version

in theaters (my first
time at the movies)
i cried in terror

for ariel, and the choice
she had to make
i knew what it meant

not to be able to speak
i know what it means
to lose a part

of yourself on purpose
i didn't like
the disney version

preferred my princess
silent like me
then sinking back

into the waves in
the end, becoming
sea foam

it just seemed
to make more sense
if my childhood

taught me anything
it taught me
that the lie in happily

ever after is not
the happiness
children shouldn't

have to think about
real endings maybe
but once they do

they can't find comfort
in happy ones
those characters

just haven't reached
the ending yet
the other shoe

will always drop
given enough time
give me an ending

that's final. skip forward
a decade to Sexton
& Plath. skip forward

another to becoming
the miracle
skip forward to thirty

and still walking
on knives still
struggling

to speak. if we are
stories we tell
ourselves, and i

have told myself
this version
for so long, how

do i stop? she says
you're a part of me
now, but what

about the parts
that will not
accept you

that want you & want
you to leave because
that's how i believe

the story ends, again
and again until
i sink back into

the sea. i want to know how
to change the story
i want not to want

to be waterlogged
or waiting for it
i dream that i am

floating, and it gives
me hope. i feel
myself being held

and i don't imagine
the end. end my books
on hopeful poems

because i want
to change the story
because i know

i am the story, if i
can only write it,
and believe.

SLAA IS FOR LOVERS

the speaker on the flier
for the conference on
your phone is saying
"MAKE CHANGE WORK FOR YOU"

and i will. i love change so much
i'm re-naming it "sex"
my five year plan is accruing
interest. it is now a five year

thirty-eight week and
five day plan, and counting.
aging is going to be great,
i mean, it's going great.

my thirties are so much better
than my twenties in that
who gives a fuck' told the chef
at the restaurant i would spend

my day off doing netflix and
nothing and forgot to do
either but wrote about my
mental health on facebook

that local graffiti artist
keeps tagging everything
'CAN WE CALL THIS LIFE'
& hard same. and big

mood. and i don't know
i just fucking agree.
lin-manuel asks
how do you write like you're

running out of time
and i guess i'm just saying
i wasn't aware that there
were other ways to write

and i guess i'm just saying
we literally are, and i guess
i'm just saying what are you up to
and you're saying 'is this foreplay'

and i'm saying yes
and i'm saying yes
and i'm saying yes.

OMG, iii.

why is anything happening
at any given moment

why do i always long
for your hands

this could be the way
the world ends

and I just want to say

okay

and mean it

IF YOU WANT TO MAKE IT STOP, THEN STOP

some things you can't confess
to yr lover so you go
to see a therapist

some things you can't confess
to yr therapist
so you go to the basement
of a church

some things you can't confess
to a room full of strangers
so you go to yr empty bedroom

some things you can't confess
to yrself & you know
where that leads, don't you

what are the right words for
this kind of aching
this buzzing at the back
of the throat?

i thought if i said the right
words in a certain order
it would break a spell, but all
it did was burn a bridge

i thought burning a bridge
would break a spell
but all it did was cut a path

i thought if i could see
my way then i could
see my way out but i didn't
have the strength

or maybe i didn't believe
hard enough or maybe
i was afraid of what i thought
i'd be losing

i like to think i know
about emptiness
but there is always farther
to fall, & i have not run
out of bridges yet

but someday i will be
too tired to build them

& the church basement
will be flooded
& i won't remember
how it got that way

or what it was that
i thought i needed
so badly to confess

FOR ALL THE TIMES I WANTED TO GIVE UP ON MYSELF

for the time i was hospitalized
& missed the first semester

of my senior year of college
for which i blamed myself

because i did not listen
to my psychiatrist when she tried

to warn me that i seemed manic
for the time i compared myself

to my college boyfriend & his
buddies hired by graduation

into finance jobs & living in
the west village at 22. for the time

i felt certain i'd made a horrible
mistake trying to do what

i loved. for the time i blamed
my mother for encouraging me

to write. for the time she had
to physically hold me down

between doses of clonazepam
& it took a long time for me to see

that this too was an act of love.
for the time i stopped taking

my medication & the years it took
to come back from the fallout

for the time i thought i'd finally
landed the kind of job i should have

& couldn't love or keep it. for the time
a friend beat his partner in front

of me & i learned what post-
traumatic stress can do to a body

for the times the depression
got so bad i stopped eating

for the things i let men do to me
because i didn't think

it mattered. i have gotten so used
to apologizing that i'm tempted

here to apologize to myself
when i know i should be saying

thank you. this is still
a work in progress.

there are still days i want
very badly to give up.

but sometimes the light
breaks through enough

for me to feel gratitude for all
the times i didn't.

and today there is, incredibly,
an abundance of light.

in view of which, i write
to myself at fifteen,

nineteen, twenty-one,
twenty-seven,

to tell her i am so grateful
that she hoped

for better, that she waited
in the dark for things

she had no certainty
would ever come

but which somehow, eventually
did, and which, most

incredibly, i am still here
to see. i don't know what to do

with joy most of the time,
can do little more than

identify it, but it is never lost
on me that i have been given

the chance to try to learn.

THRESHOLD OF REVELATION

yes, some days it has felt
like for every door i opened
three closed behind me

i've just always known it was
never an option
not to open that door.

broken as i thought
myself to be, even i knew
that to stop opening doors
was death

& as hard as i may, at times,
have wanted this all to end,   ·

holding a gun in your hand
is entirely a different thing
than pulling a trigger.

CHOOSE YOUR OWN BEGINNING

it would never be enough
to be in love by itself

but it is still so good
i kiss your hands in the dream

i kiss your hands while you are sleeping
and never take it back

take the flowers from my hair
put me back in the earth

where i always wanted to be

IF I TELL YOU I LOVE YOU

i'm not trying to keep you
i say, nestled against
your shoulder, and you

laugh, say *as you nakedly*
cuddle. it is not
your day off but mine

this is not   my home
but yours but i
have been here for so

long, and how do you
not make yourself
at home in all that time

siken writes, *everyone*
needs a place. it
shouldn't be inside

of someone else. but god
does it feel good
not to be alone sometimes

flanked by small
dependent animals
reluctantly sharing

the bed with one another
to be within

arm's reach of us

i think how all of us need
so badly
to be touched

as soon as i feel
your body begin
to rise i will lift

my head from
your chest
unlatch my arm

and let go
but if you were
hoping i

would make the first
move toward
the rest of the day

oh honey, i'm sorry
you should
have known better

and i have no interest
in being
your small dependent

animal. and if one day
you are not here
to touch me someone

will take your place
and you
are not even

my home but this
is not your
day off, it's mine

and when you
move for
the door to start

your day, i will
tell you
goodbye

but while you are
still within
arm's reach

i will not deny
myself
another moment

i'm not trying
to keep you
but if you were

expecting me
to help
you leave,

oh honey,
i'm
sorry.

TBH

sometimes i hear your voice
in my head when i write now

i just want you to be okay
is what i tell myself

if you love someone enough
they become a part of you

this is all i want to do
for the rest of my life

I LOVE YOU AND

it doesn't make
anything better
and it makes
everything better

and i guess that's
why i do it

also because
of the little way
you growl
when you're annoyed

and every time
you've ever kissed
my forehead

VIRGO SEASON

the other night
asleep in
your arms

i dreamt that we
were dancing

in the dream
i was warm
and blissfully
happy

i remember
shifting
positions—

my cheek on
your chest,
your arms
around
my waist

and half-
waking then
drifting
back

usually,
my dreams
range

from neutral
to nightmare

i think
i must have
forgotten

the word for
the opposite
of nightmare

then remember
that it is just 'dream'

i've never needed
to invent
a new language

but i guess
there is
a first time

for everything

because this
is what i do

and i don't
have words
for what

i've never
had
to describe

i haven't
been writing
lately

and i thought
it was because
i was too tired

but the thought
before the thought

was that to write
about my joy

was dangerous

not worth the risk
of scaring it off

but now i think
life is
so short

and for people
like me, joy
is so rare

and this
is what i do

and i still
don't have
the words

and it would
be easier
to write

my grief
forever
but grief

that goes
on forever
eventually

stops being
grief

and, as you

and i keep
saying, this

is virgo
season

why would
we choose

what's easy
for ease's
sake

and maybe joy
that is
hardest won

is most
powerful

and if i have
to invent
a new language

to be happy
i think it will still

be worth
every word.

TOUCH THE SKY

not because
we're running out
of time
but because
we can
start to see it
passing

not that we'll die
without it
but that
you never know
until it's
too late

i can picture
everyone i've
ever loved
but not
as they are now

i text a man i think
i wronged years ago
to apologize

while i thought
he hated me,
he'd assumed
i hated him

imagine
a love story
that is just
two people
apologizing
to each other
endlessly

now imagine one
that isn't

6/9/2020

it is the first day
of my so-called Jesus year
but i have only

prayed twice in my life
and i suspect

some things are not meant
to be saved.

my mother cannot throw
anything away.

when she and my aunt
cleaned out
their parents' house

April packed up
every last effect into
the Honda,

even my grandfather's
old boxers, and
now they are in a rented

storage space with
the records
no one wanted.

i am shocked
when she tells me
the monthly fee

to store all of it
but i suppose
i shouldn't be.

there's always
a cost
to holding

onto things:
old nightgowns,
cruel lovers.

the ways in which
the things we cling to
weigh us down.

Marie Kondo says
if it doesn't
spark joy, let it go

and i am no
minimalist
but I think

she has a point.
I cannot make
my mother leave

her angry boy-
friend but
someday

i will have
to clean out
her house

and i think
i am reaching
the age

when you start
to feel how finite
this all is

and you think
you'd better know
what kind

of person
you're going to be.
my mother

takes thousands
of photographs
amassing archives

of moments
that will now exist
in a way, forever

i try to distill
every feeling
down to

its essence
strip myself layer
by layer

i am now
a year older
than my

mom was
when
she had me

i suppose
it is easy
for me, with

no husband
or children

to preach
feeling untethered

but i'm going
to do it anyway:

there is nothing
more important in
the world

than freedom.
you can only hold
so much

and still
move comfortably.

if doesn't spark joy,
you should probably
strongly consider

letting it go.

THE GREAT POEM OF MY LOVE FOR YOU

is not a poem
at all

i sing
to myself in
the morning

when i have
the strength

loving you
does not give
me strength

it is strength
that allows
me to do it

but oh how
much stronger

i feel
when i am able
to sing

oh how much
stronger
i know that i am

in my capacity
for love

we talk now
of what
our public

servants owe us
or don't

i wash
my hands until
my skin

becomes raw

i don't owe
you anything

but still i give
you love

nobody owes
anyone
anything

that's why
it is so
extraordinary

when
they give it

ON HAVING BEEN IN LOVE FOR NEARLY HALF MY LIFE

not always with the same man
but always with the same terror
the same tenderness and fear
finally giving way to not-fear
until the floor drops out
beneath me and the wound opens again

the thing about having been
abandoned is
it never really goes away
the thing about having been
abandoned is you always are

except for the sweet stretches
in between when you are
trying so hard not to hold on
so tightly that you crush it
trying so hard that your muscles
that have been tense so long
start to relax trying so hard
that you almost stop having to

and sometimes the stretches
are brief and they never seem
to be long enough and some days
even in the sweetest center
of the best stretch the wind rushes in
and you remember that somewhere
you are still hollow
and somewhere you are still small
and somewhere you are still
on the floor of your childhood bedroom
wrapped in a ball even while you are
in the arms of the person you love

and you think if you are enveloped
completely enough
and you think if you are loved enough
one day you will wake up
and the fear will not only be gone
in the morning but it won't
be back by the end of the day
or the week or the month

so you wait for that day to arrive
and you wait for that day to arrive
and you wait for that day to arrive

but in the meantime
maybe you plant flowers

and in the meantime
maybe you have children

and in the meantime
you say goodbye
to your parents

and one day you wake up
and you have spent almost
your entire life in love

and maybe the fear is still there
maybe it never went away

but maybe your child doesn't
inherit the whole of it

and maybe the image
of your small self
wrapped in your own arms

is still there and you will
never forget her
or take away her pain

but your child doesn't
inherit the whole of it

and you look at your life
stretched out now behind you
and there has been so much love
that it is almost all
you remember

and you pray that your child
inherits all of it

and she does.

ACKNOWLEDGMENTS

grateful to *American Poetry Review, Luna Luna Magazine, The Rumpus, GlitterMOB, The Tiny, Queen Mob's Teahouse, Silent Auctions, Bedfellows,* and *Wax Nine* for publishing some of these poems.

to Alexandra Naughton, Michael J. Seidlinger, Janice Lee, Monica McClure, Ben Fama, Liz Bowen, Joanna C. Valente, Kay Sorin, Alina Pleskova, Raena Shirali, Cayla Lockwood, Christina Rosso-Schneider, D. Ted Tarnovski, Sarah Rose Etter, Jaime Fountaine, Mike Ingram, Anthony Torcasio, Sean Lynch, David Hancock, Brooke & Anthony Palma, Zach Blackwood, Faye Chevalier, Itiola Jones, Logen Cure, Jamie Mortara, Marisa Siegel, Cortney Lamar Charleston, Savannah Cooper-Ramsey, Austin Islam, Prairie M. Faul, June Gehringer, Dave Kiefaber, Bud Smith, Derrick C. Brown, Noah Cicero, Richie Hofmann, Rachelle Toarmino, Nariya Lofton, and Dylan Allen for their support of me and my work.

to Shy, Jennie, Angelo, Brianna & Nishit for their friendship; to Eric for his love and support; and to my mother and sister for everything

AMY SAUL-ZERBY is the author of two previous poetry collections, *Paper Flowers Imaginary Birds* and *Deep Camouflage*. Her poems have appeared in The Rumpus, The Chicago Review of Books, American Poetry Review, Painted Bride Quarterly, and elsewhere. She edits *Voicemail Poems*.

MORE TITLES FROM BE ABOUT IT PRESS

- *I've Been On Tumblr* by Jesse Prado, 2014
- *Bye, Product* by Catch Breath, 2015
- *Paper Flowers, Imaginary Birds* by Amy Saul-Zerby, 2017
- *I Love You, It Looks Like Rain* by June Gehringer, 2018
- *Disaster Horse: Smol Essays* by Nooks Krannie, 2019
- *A Pretty Little Wilderness* by Cassandra Dallett, 2020
- *Be A Bough Tit* by Richard Loranger, 2020
- *Double Rainbow* by Lonely Christopher, 2021
- *Blueberry Lemonade* by Marzi Margo, 2021
- *Broken: A Life of Aileen Wuornos in 33 Poems* by Natasha Dennerstein, 2021
- *Emoji Revival* by Marzi Margo, 2022

Find out more on our website! beaboutitpress.com
Follow @baipress on twitter

Made in USA - Crawfordsville, IN
79503_9780998601281
12.07.2022 1418